Walking Sweetly

Lio Spinelli

First edition.

Published by MOJO Media Insights, Brighton.

Typeset in Century Schoolbook.

Front cover image by Penny Roberts.
Back cover image by Becky Hallet.

Copyright Lio Spinelli 2019, who asserts his moral rights as author.

Dedicated to you, the reader, to all young people working hard at and believing in their own recoveries, and to all the therapists, nurses and doctors who have helped me on my way.

Table of Contents

Introduction	6
A Simple Gesture	8
What I Have	9
Ouch	10
Your Power	11
Exercise	12
Another Day	13
The Man in the Field	14
Feel	17
Under the Bridge	18
Goodnight the Moon	19
First October Days	20
Joys	24
Dew	25
Busy Streets of Calm Spring	26
Smile	27
Keep On Keeping On	28
Being	29
Conjugations of Beauty	30
Through Open Windows	31
You Are the Generation	32
It Will Be Morning Again	34
Untitled	35
Young Men	36
Structure	37
Dark Veil	38
Long Walks	39
In the End You Will	40
Poem in Exams	41

Old Men Walk	42
Peace and Happiness	44
Bliss Is To See Dawn	45
Shall I Go Till the End of the Day	46
The Alpha State	47
Reflections	48
Beyond the Fog	49
Smoke	50
An Evening in April, or Just Back from the Maldoons'	51

Introduction

While I can't *feel* your injury, sickness or pain directly, I know it hurts and I know you'd rather be someplace else.

I first started writing poetry after I saw the film *Paterson* by Jim Jarmusch (2016). If you have the mildest interest in literature and art, it's worth a watch.

It tells the story of an incredibly down-to-earth bus driver named Paterson. Paterson happens to live and work in the town of Paterson, New Jersey, and he loves reading the "imagist" poet William Carlos Williams (who lived in the same town). He also writes little poems that help him escape the mundaneness of his working life.

Like Paterson, I write poems that try to see the beauty in simple little things. I also write poems to help me think about bigger, abstract things and to help me gain a bit of power over the stuff that seems out of control. That's helped me deal with things and helped change my perspective on things and keep me positive, which is good medicine.

I hope this small book is read by young people in similar situations, maybe on hospital wards, or trying to get themselves through injuries and illnesses, physical and mental, at home.

Four years after watching *Paterson*, I was again on a hospital ward (Coxen Ward at the Royal National Orthopaedic Hospital in London) talking about the poetry on the walls with the play therapist Michelle Sicheri. It was in that moment that I got inspired to produce *Walking Sweetly*. I hope it helps you as much as it did me.

A Simple Gesture

A simple gesture,
That shows all in one.
Like a child guiding a blind man
Across a busy New York street.

And the man gets tired,
And asks the boy, "Can I sit down?"

They walk across the white lines
With green men—flashing numbers.
The men stop flashing,
And go red.
Still with lines to cross,
On a busy New York street,
The cab waits.
A simple gesture.
Blind—unique and impenetrable.
And then
After they cross
The cab goes
With distant drums and voices.

What I Have

I have what I have,
And what I have is special.
Like the saying at the end of the day:
"I am *still* alive."
You can't commodify that.
The memories of scenarios, on that
    particular day.
The *people* who were in that day.
The people.

I have who I have in my life,
And they are all unique.
I all care for them and
They all care for me.
Care—The most valuable thing on the
    planet.

I am who I am,
A boy, a man, a son. I know who I am,
I know what I am and what I have.
That knowing is rare.

I have lost what I have lost,
And sad I have been
Because of that loss.
But I will have what Life throws at me,
And how I throw it back,
Is Carpe Diem.

Ouch

Where pain burns fire,
And water can't simmer it.
Eyes, so innocent and articulate in pain.
Bloom in anatomical truth.

Your Power

Go to the table,
And sit on a chair.
Get a pen and paper,
And write.

Exercise

Wear—clothes.
Hospital gowns, mesh—no pants,
bandages to corner
A better you—you are not beaten but
    beat.
Hospitals do not and cannot beat you,
But leave you beat.
Beat as in tired and weary.
And very weak and dreary.

Weakness is not your having been
    beaten,
But an opportunity for you to engage
    with yourself—beat.
You have the eye,
That beats beat itself.
The eye of the tiger.
There's probably one on a wall in the
    ward.
Smiling above you, with its eyes.
Fueling – your – eyes.
To exercise.

Exercise in free moments,
Moments of youth and support.
Serenity can motivate,
But the Eye of the Tiger, man.
And the shake of joy.

Another Day

I sit here, and look,
For that day to arrive.
When I get out of that wheelchair,
And stand up, and walk.

Waiting, in the lonely place of
discrepancy,
For my right leg to grow.
Lonely—yet how beautiful it all is,
As I am lucky, with what I know.

I am here, and here I will stay.
I'm with that.

The Man in the Field

I sit in the tree
Clinging as it sways
Bent, left and right
As it is shattered.

The wind that blows
Against my face,
That is cold,
And leaves it battered.

I am the unspoken word,
That clings to every leaf,
They crave the lost air
Among their fellow partners.

The sky that dwindles
And the earth that sets in the outcoming
 of that.
I am their sky, day and night
I feel little.

My friend: The brick,
That cries at every passing voice that
bludgeons the vulnerable.
I am there too.
I am *there* with the brick that cries at
 humanity, for all the darkness
 that it has shed,
Across the land and sea.

We cry at moments when meaningful

      souls meet,
At the happiness and joy, we feel when
      they greet.
And strength when they stand with
      their hearts and not their feet.
The strength grows and multiplies, like
      togethering wheat.

Anyway —
Like silk, I see dreams rise,
As they blanket my sky, in
      unpracticalized tomorrows.
They dream solely to realize what they
      can do,
Their dream is not as sweet
      as the realization of their
      potential.
Their apex of night,
While I — Being who I am,
Am bound to a tree, in evening night,
As the persistent dream their dreams
      right,
And when they awake, they carry on
      that dreams light,
They realize their potential, that they
      saw on that cold, evening night.

I feel my cold, my own doing,
Against my warm feet,
That *sweat* in midnight dew.

I laugh a little.
Only subtle though,

Like prisoners singing Johnny Cash.
In harmonies of triumph,
Blended in inequity.

I cry a little now,
A mild whimper — But out of joy.
I see yellow and orange,
Rise in East from a growing hemisphere,
This is why I cry —
Because this is *making* today,
    from dreams.
Tears wet my cheeks

In time of death.
I am Frost, and I will melt.
In warmth and in Beauty —
I die.
And my wet tears,
Crystallise
And form a crisp layer, in the fields.
I will come back.
Like the Butterfly.

Feel

Feel the clothing on your chest,
And the shoes that protect your
Feet from the rough ground.
Clothes keep you warm,
They keep the cold air from getting to
    you.
Shoes allow you to walk free from
Discomfort.
Those of you who currently have one,
Feel their warm hand on your chest,
Feel their palm against your palm,
Exchanging warmth in the cold.

Under the Bridge

Under the bridge,
There is still current,
and the water still flows.
The birds still fly,
And the wind still blows.
Under the bridge, there is still current.

The current is still water,
And water that moves.
Above the ground and below the air,
It is still water that moves.
It looks like a glazing of the ground.

You are both under the bridge,
and over the bridge,
You are in the water,
looking.
And you are looking out
from the water itself,
At yourself,
At your looking.

If you are in the water,
Under the bridge,
You too are above the bridge.
Like a mirror,
You see your reflection,
In the moving current,
Under the bridge.

And if you really are:
Under the bridge,
Think again.

Goodnight the Moon

For this place I'm about to describe,
There is no sound of the modern world,
Just the sound of crickets;
Humming faintly.
Or that of people   screaming into their
         technology;
Just the sound of Eva's laugh,
and two women,
speaking a language I don't understand.

For this place I'm about to describe,
There are no cars or street lamps,
Just trees in brown dust,
Behind an amber sky,
And fading mountain crests.

For this place I'm about to describe,
The moon's pupil looks up,
And the whites of its eye
         shine bright,
Under the dancing lights.
Goodnight the moon.

First October Days

  5th October/22:55

The October sky is a beauty,
When the tramontuous hours begin.
And the setting sun, is so including,
As it shines on the corner bin.

And I stand there, being vulnerable,
And innocent too.
Amongst these beautiful creations,
The blue sky, the orange clouds,
The yellow sun, and all this is true.

They are real in their presence,
And overwhelmingly so.
As there is so much in their essence,
And the story behind them that grows.

The story of the Apple Tree,
That stands in the lit garden.
Before the brick wall, and after me,
The day grows older, it does happen.

  6th October/22:45

How innocent is the Apple Tree,
Carrying on with no leaves.
And the poorest of branches: At the top,
Looking on the nostalgia of Spring.

Where leaves were green,
And the branches: High.
And life, its consistency unseen,
But now the leaves do lie.

On the ground where grass is,
Soaking up leaves' tears.
As if soldiers in War,
Battling their reluctancy.

But leaves do lie, in Flanders Fields,
As their tree, being their life.
And as its flowers have ceased to bud,
They fall, in their longest proxemics.

But their corpse is still there,
And shall never die.
Their corpse: The Trunk,
Knows Spring will arrive.

As it is reminded by its only hope,
Its hymn: Sung by the flying Bugles.
This string of hope in posterity.
Carries it on through Fall and Winter.

But this song does not ring on the 11th
    minute,
But sounds from above.
Moves in space, and in sky.
Like the sounding of persistent
livelihood.

The hymn: The birds' songs,
Saying: *'Death is not the end my friend'.*
It echoes in perfect oscillation.
In wind, in storm, in modernism,
It is understood by nature.

      7th October/22:10

The wind blows past the trunk,
"You can still feel me." Wind says.
And moves along. *"I can still feel you."*
The trunk replies, with dignity in its
    roots.

Each leaf, colouring the ground in brown
    and red.
The blood, of the unbeaten soldier, does
    what it does best: Colours
the earth in militaristic truth,
As it draws parallels with the beauty of
    realism.

Autumn is beautiful,
The Birds sing arias to grounded trees.
The floor is colourful,
With red and brown leaves.

I feel the cool wind
Moving past me: Stutterless.
I am alive, I can conceptualize
the beauty of Autumn.
Anyone who is alive can do so.

And above me,
I see orange, blooming with red, blue,
and yellow. The clouds, the sky
and the tree, are all alive in
the light's vibrant glow.

The clouds, they move,
The birds, do sing.
The wind does blow,
All on metaphysical terms.
And more: can nature have all these
        things, and perform to its greatest,
yet perfectly mild amount of eccentricity.

Grass still blooms,
With unstructured and unamounted
        colour.
The leaves fall on the ground.

And though the blood has spread along
        the grassy floor,
The Bugle still sounds, as it flies,
the wind still blows, and the sun still
        shines.

I am there,
Watching it all, as it digresses in
the asymmetrical charm of Fall.

Joys

Joys, of like a turtle, engaged in its
Age like a swimmer swims,
The turtle thinks as its shell,
Difficult and hard,
Breaks the water to breathe, fine air,
Small again in, and the water falls
From her eyes, opening small,
In two worlds.
Matrices of abandonment
And blue sky with white black birds
Feathers grey across air
In clouds.
Breathing alive,
—like others that love in,
and out,
There is always love.

Dew

Dew
On morning green,
In the early hours,
Of the birds' songs,
And the sky
A darkish blue,
Waits for yellow.

Busy Streets of Calm Spring

Busy streets of calm spring,
Where love is made
Flowers bud,
And the grass grows
And the birds chirp
In the busy streets of the calm spring.

Love is made
Under branches low and high,
Always breathing in air from the leaves,
Breathing out our air for the trees.
Memories grasp is of one's first kiss,
Under wooden branches,
In spring air.

Flowers bud, on branches' end.
Casting the shade of a few
On kissing faces.
Flowers bud,
In the grass.
A lone and beautiful thing,
And, together, beautiful things.
You never see a green flower,
They exist to colour what's already there,
In the grass,
Like the kisses of—
In love.
The field is already there,
Love is,
The grass always grows,
As the tree will,
And the flowers will come,
Like the kiss.

Smile

The beauty of a smile
Is its intention
To make better your day,
And to house the emotion of love
In our hearts.

So easy it is to smile,
And so much can it be in my day.
Like watching a shooting star,
In its last moments before leaving the
    sky.

Keep On Keeping On

Keep on keeping on,
As all good teachers say.
And when it gets tough and tiring,
Remember that you're alive,
Today.

When the path inclines,
Do, Not, Back, Down!
Hold yourself tight and keep who you
      are,
While your feet,
Meet and leave
The ground.

When you finish
Your incline,
Look back,
So.

Why did you climb?
Look forward, look up,
Look at what you couldn't
See from below.

Being

If I see,
I'm lucky.
If I hear,
I'm lucky.
If I feel,
I'm lucky.
If I taste,
I'm lucky.
If I smell,
I'm lucky.
If I can do any of these things,
I am.

Conjugations of Beauty

Listen
Words are speaking—out mouths
Made by words
Made of meaning.
Listen to where words breathe—and
      yet—
There is no account in words,
Only those who speak the words.
But their mouths are no account.
Yes, it may kiss different to yours—
It may be bigger than yours—
It may speak more than yours,
But in terms of meaning—
Is that *really* what speech is?
A sound in a note—
Like the speed of a flying bird.
The peregrine falcon flies at 390km an
      hour.
What would that be in speech?

Through Open Windows

Windows look at you.
They tell you
That you're strong,
That you're resistant.
And they remind you that you are
 human.
You *feel* pain—
The window knows, and it sees.

You Are the Generation

You are the generation,
That falls behind.
You are the generation,
That stands alone.

You are a generation,
With hearts and minds.
And yet you use them,
To knock down others' bones.

You are the generation,
That laughs at madness.
You are the generation,
That curses and swears.

You are the generation,
That supports crudeness.
I am telling you now,
Someone will stare.

You, the people have the power
To change; we all do.

At your petty remarks,
Of your unacquainted dignity
In the countless hands
Too strong, yet too weak, you are the
    generation.

You are the generation,
That talks aloud,

Within your countless heads,
To attain full dignity.

You are the generation,
That is lost in the crowd.
You are the generation,
That seeks someone's validity.

You are the generation,
That grows on others' power.
Yet you stop to find,
What you have in common.

You are the generation,
That can change skies into stars,
Moons into suns,
And tears into smiles.

You are the generation,
That has power to change.
You, the people,
We: Humanity.

You are the generation,
That can make anything possible.
That can change possible into definite,
Because we are the generation.

It Will Be Morning Again

Remember this when all is grey,
And the birds don't sing,
And the children don't play.

Remember this when the pain gets worse,
And the children cry aloud.
Tomorrow may be, but today comes first,
And together, the days do crowd.

It will be *morning* again!

Untitled

The art on your bedside table is unique,
Because it is for *you*.
Your favourite.

Young Men

I see young men,
Who have dreams and powers.
To manifest those dreams,
Yet they seem to take hours.

Let them be—boys with dreams.
And let them go—boys with dreams.
It takes time to make those dreams,
And time means they won't come true.

I see young men,
Who have dreams and will
Reach those dreams and then
They line their lives with dreams until—

I see old men,
Who have made themselves happy
Because when they were young,
Their dreams were reality.

Structure

Keep moving towards what gives you a
      reason,
Don't let yourself get detached
From what motivates you... to move.
Let all who you come by know that you
      do.
Do not text this,
Show this!
Move to the sun that shines in your dark,
Stare at the light it provides, and
      remember what you felt.

Dark Veil

The night's grey dark veil under knives
    sees no stars
To shine along in shapes and shining.
Understand you.
From encumbered skies so far that you
don't notice the sky itself.
Not a dark, but nihilism.
Yet nihilism itself is a belief.
Believe in the grey dark veil,
From its mix of colour,
Unseen potential.

Long Walks

I have walked long walks
With my friends after school,
Climbing green hills
And swimming in blue pools.
I have laughed out loud,
I have smiled because I have laughed
And until that opportunity came to be
I had to be positive
For my surgery.

Just think for a moment—
Of all those times
You've tripped over rocks—
Into green-earth thyme.

When all this is over,
Walk long walks, laugh out loud, and cry.
Like the birds, in what they see,
In flight.

In the End You Will

The road is hard
But it is still solid ground.
The day is long,
But beginning and an end.

Love isn't sadness,
It's the emotion that is sown within us—
That dwells in every heart and every
      mind.
Love isn't sadness. It is happiness.

She is my pen that I hold in my hand,
And he is the ink that is let out in words.
You are the paper that disperses this ink,
And I am the brain that holds
everything else.

You are my mind,
You are my soul,
You are my—

You healed me
When I was in pain.
You comforted me
Through my difficult days.

You ran beside me,
When I was struggling.
You nurtured me,
Through hunger and thirst.

Poem in Exams

Rows of chairs, and columns of minds,
Do what minds do, and have done for a long time.
They try, and they succeed—some do and some don't.
They wait until the bell goes, or a clock strikes noon.

Scribbles of ink, and erased pencil markings,
Do what they do, in black or white.
That is all they see,
And numbers on a page, is whatever life will be.

It is wrong.
It is right.
Like day.
Like night.

Maybe.

Old Men Walk

Old men walk,
With three legs and a beard.
As they grow older,
Age compresses them.
As age walks them to sleep,
Where no legs need no feet.
They walk asleep to dawn light,
And you are left there to weep.
Do not weep so much,
As to cry of death.
For life is such,
Under your breath,
A gift in itself,
A gift.
You cry and you weep,
For the rich and the meek
For the strong and the week.
You cry and you weep;
I thank who is there,
And the clouds above.
The night smothers wrath and tears,
And the people who are there
Console me.

I look to the sun,
And weep to the moon,
And look to the stars
Where old men lay.

Where old men lay,
They smile on me

They smile on you too,
It's there, in them.

I am rich when you smile
I am poor when you don't.
All I want is a smile.

Peace and Happiness

He thanks the strengths that hold him,
Tight from temptatious sin.
Deep in the fields of blood and wrath,
Where no weapon nor man can win.

He thanks his mind that leads him,
To peace and happiness alike.
Through the bitterness in knowledge,
and the scarceness of days,
He's afraid of death in the night.

For death in the night he fears,
As he doesn't want to go unknown.
As for many this is the case,
As for many, they go alone.

But he is not one of them,
He does not fight in fields of blood.
Nor does he venture in them,
But peace and happiness he yields.

And then one evening he wakes up,
And walks / into a run.
We don't know where he *ran* to,
But we know he left in the sun.

Bliss Is To See Dawn

Why mourn to see the sun too bright?
The cryings blemish each starry night.
Why want to see, whose joy is dust?
To those of you, whose life is thirst.

But cry for those whose blindness sees,
The beauty of stars, and the beauty of we.
For they see life, as pure and sweet,
And don't retreat, to blackened defeats.

For that lets them, to carry on,
Deep into the night, where peace is won.
Where blackened defeats, have no right,
To label them, as fear of fight.

The stars and the skies, do all to shine,
Beyond sweet tears, and taste of wine.
Nurturing of boys, to crave withdrawals,
Bliss is to see dawn.

Shall I Go Till the End of the Day

I shall go till the end of the day,
When the night smothers me.
My exams; Be them what they may,
I shall go till the end of the day.

Upon the light that kisses me,
The moon, she is my owl.
That knows what tomorrow's pains may be,
Where Triumph and Glory are that hour.

My soul does not stoop,
Nor shudder in fear.
My mind cannot droop,
And my eyes do not tear.

For I have felt triumphant wins,
And focused on their loom
My success, I have dinned,
As it grew in the womb.

So I will sit in my seat,
And answer, unafraid.
Be still with my feet,
Fearful pasts have today made.

Black is the night that smothers me,
And darkness, is the way.
Let me be what I may be,
I shall go till the end of the day.

The Alpha State

At 7, the birds do fly,
Beneath a light blue sky.
And the clouds: White, and large.
In nature, stretching beyond empirical
    metrics.

The sound of cars passing by, as if
questioning your engagement
    in nature—
Your attachment with nature.
If it has distracted you, you hadn't yet
    entered the Alpha State,
And all this being,
Gazed upon by the half-moon
in the sky.
And a bright star,
Small and to the moon's 10 o'clock.
Keeping your reality sane.

Reflections

Where childish smiles envelope
    nostalgia,
And tears of the past, come to the
    present.
And their warmth, You feel as they
stutter down your face,
Like leaves in Autumn air.
The tree is your face,
And mood be four seasons.
Leaves can be those tears,
And also the face of the mood.

And the mirror sees all this—
Tears gathering at the chin,
Red eyes, that glow in progressive
    transparency.
If the mirror could feel, its life lays its
dependency on you and your
    seasons of mood.

And if crying is all your mood does
exploit,
    How violent you are with such a
natural innocence—Your reflection.

Let it see joy, and thus be joyous.

Beyond the Fog

Foggy windows

In the rain
> On one side of the glass,
> Is you,
> And all you see,
> Is without you,
> But how you see — is from within
> > you.
> If you look at a single-glaze in the
> > cold,
> It's foggy, or droplets of water
> > have formed.

> Press a finger or palm onto the
> wet glass,
> and you'll see streams
> tearing through the fog, and
> > parting it aside,
> so you can see what's beyond the
> > fog.

Smoke

Barbecue smoke
Distantly recognized.
The smell of trees, asleep.
Following the road,
Of quiet ears,
Of moss
Growing
Between
Brick-walled bricks.
Feeling the uneven
As you pass your fingers,
V
e
r
t
i
c
a
l
l
y.

An Evening in April, or Just Back from the Maldoons'

Soft
Scented
Spray sprays along invisible clouds,
Beneath the bright stars,
Shining Easter's birth.
----
maybe the poem ends <u>here</u>.

www.ingramcontent.com/pod-product-compliance
Lightning Source LLC
Chambersburg PA
CBHW062205100526
44589CB00014B/1957